The Return

Selected Poems

T0243333

Myfanwy Haycock (1913-1963) was one of the Eastern Valley of Wales's most endearing and talented female lyric poets, publishing seven poetry collections and broadcasting her poems on radio and television.

In 1932, Haycock won the English Lyric entry at the National Eisteddfod, Port Talbot, for her poem 'The Hill of Dreams' and, later, two bardic chairs, at Ebbw Vale and Newport. Her poetry embodied her love of nature, places, and her hometown of Pontypool. She was a regular feature writer for the *South Wales Argus*, *Western Mail* and many other publications; illustrating her poems and short stories with scraperboard woodcuts. Moving to London in 1943, she worked for the BBC and became a member of The Society of Women Writers and Journalists.

Haycock was the youngest of three daughters born in Pontnewynydd to coalminer James David Haycock and his wife Alice Maud. In 1947, she married Dr Arthur Williams, settling in Surrey with three children. At the age of fifty, she tragically passed away after a debilitating illness.

The Return

Selected Poems

Myfanwy Haycock

Edited with an introduction by Jenni Crane

Parthian, Cardigan SA43 1ED
www.parthianbooks.com
First published in 2023
© Estate of Myfanwy Haycock 2023
ISBN 978-1-914595-88-2
Editor: Jenni Crane
Cover image: 'Fantasy' by Myfanwy Haycock (1937)
Cover design by www.theundercard.co.uk
Typeset by Elaine Sharples
Printed and bound by 4edge Limited, UK
Published with the financial support of the Welsh Books Council
British Library Cataloguing in Publication Data
A cataloguing record for this book is available from the British Library
Printed on FSC accredited paper

Contents

from **THE MYFANWY HAYCOCK POETRY TRAIL (2023)**

Artwork
Acknowledgements

Introduction

There are certain people in life with whom – for some unknown reason – you feel an affinity. To me, Myfanwy Haycock is one of these. My first memory of Myfanwy remains as vivid now as it did when I discovered her poetry thirty years ago. I was eight years old and my dad, a local author writing a book about our hometown, Pontypool, had met with Gwladys Haycock, Myfanwy's sister. She gave him a copy of *Hill of Dreams* and on returning home, my dad gave it to me. I sat on the floor in front of the fire in my parents' dining room motionless, transfixed, reading, then re-reading her words. They floated off the page and swirled around my head – new rhyme, new words, new worlds – new visions of home and a dream born.

Born in Pontnewynydd, Pontypool in 1913, Myfanwy carved out a career through World War II as one of the Eastern Valley of Wales's most talented female poets, yet her story is surprisingly undiscovered. By the time she was ten years old, she had written thirty-eight poems, with illustrations. Dubbed as 'Gwent's second voice' her career took off at the age of nineteen when W. H. Davies chose her poem 'The Hill of Dreams' as the winning English lyric entry at the National Eisteddfod held at Port Talbot, in 1932. She went on to win several local bardic chairs in semi-national Eisteddfodau. Myfanwy was a skilled black and white scraperboard artist, having trained in Cardiff School of Art. However, her main medium of expression and first love was poetry. She broadcast her poems on radio, television, and worked for the BBC in London as a playwright. She was a council member of the SWWJ (Society of Women Writers and Journalists) and contributed as a features writer to the *Western Mail, South Wales Argus, Daily Sketch* and numerous other publications. She wrote short stories and seven poetry books, four of which were posthumously published, following her death, aged fifty, in 1963.

After reading her *Hill of Dreams* biography, the words that resonated and impressed me most were 'she worked for the BBC in London'. This gave me enormous hope, a self-belief and fire in my belly, that beyond Pontypool, dreams could be made in London. I didn't give much consideration to her being fifty at the time of her death. This part was wasted on my youth – ignorance is bliss! The places that she wrote about were all on my doorstep, one being the Folly Tower, which had been reduced to a pile of stones in World War Two to avoid it serving as an aerial landmark for German bombers seeking out the nearby munitions factory. The wise old 'Tower of Strength' on a *Hill of Dreams* lived on in Myfanwy's poetry until, a local Charity named C.R.O.F.T (in which my father was a member), led a successful campaign to rebuild the old Folly. The Tower was officially re-opened on 22nd July 1994 by the former HRH The Prince of Wales, now King Charles II. I was honoured to present him with a copy of Myfanwy's *Hill of Dreams*.

I moved to London to pursue my creative dreams at The Italia Conti Academy. I was eighteen and homesick, so I took great comfort from finding one of Myfanwy's books, *Mountain over Paddington* in a Covent Garden bookshop. The majority of these poems, I had never before read. Myfanwy pours her homesick heart out as she asks a simple question; *Tell me, is there snow at home?* In the face of rejection, she unapologetically expresses her resilience in her poem 'To a Critic' and may it be said... Myfanwy had the last laugh.

Myfanwy's work exceeds any local hometown connection; her exceptional poetry transports and connects the reader back to Wales with words. With the books long out of print and inaccessible to new readers, it both concerned and saddened me to think that her work was at risk of being forgotten, before her legacy had even been fully realised and celebrated in Pontypool or indeed Wales.

After leaving drama school I landed my first job as Hermione Granger's body double in *Harry Potter and The Chamber of Secrets*. The acting roles that subsequently followed were largely dictated by my height – 4' 11". I was typecast in playing teenager roles, so I changed career direction and became a TV presenter, working on shows such as *The Wright Stuff* (Channel 5). Over the years, I realised that it was the content and stories that I cared most about and not necessarily the lure of being in front of the camera. It was from an unexpected suitcase that I found in a Crystal Palace antique shop that my career was again transformed. I received my first BBC Radio Four commission to author *The Chaplain's Suitcase* – a story of a forgotten war hero, Rev G.E.M Parry (who happened to be of Welsh origin). This gave me enormous satisfaction and in some ways, was reminiscent of Myfanwy, for she too had an untold story.

Many years later, with a career as a TV/ radio producer and the first National Welsh BBC continuity announcer, I finally began researching Myfanwy's life story. I spent countless hours delving through extensive archives at Torfaen Museum in Pontypool. The former curator Deborah Wildgust shared invaluable, personal memories of Myfanwy's doting son, Wynn and sister, Gwladys. By all accounts, Gwladys was a force to be reckoned with and had dedicated her life to keeping her sister's legacy alive. (My dad's meeting with Gwladys was fortuitous indeed).

I will never forget Deborah's warning that if I ever wrote a book, or made a programme, about Myfanwy then 'Don't forget Gwladys.'

The rich tapestry of items; old scrapbooks, radio scripts, unpublished poetry, a semi-autobiographical novel and even a rare recording on cassette, allowed me to get to know Myfanwy, the woman. I read in an old *Pontypool Free Press* article:

> Soundless the poet was not. And I suspect that as long as her poems are put before us by her sister or whoever may come after, she will never walk alone in the hearts of Gwent people.

In strong contrast to that of her poems, her outspoken, controversial articles in the *Pontypool Free Press, Western Mail* and *Daily Herald* still strike a chord today. She was ahead of her time, writing articles on strong Welsh identity, proper pronunciation, and even heated debates on sexual matters. Myfanwy called out stories that did not necessarily make headline news, such as domestic abuse, and refused to be silenced or told by any critic that her poems were 'but a weak and cowardly escape.'

2023 marks sixty years since Myfanwy died and 110 years since her birth, which feels like the most opportune time to introduce her work to a new generation. I came up with the idea of The Myfanwy Haycock Poetry Trail (MHPT) to link all of the places from which she drew poetic inspiration, with a statue and audio poetry app. Pontypool Community Council unanimously agreed to fund this important project to celebrate a former female artist. Over the past year, we have worked tirelessly to place Myfanwy markers along the eight miles of the route, taking in Pontypool Park and three miles along the Monmouthshire & Brecon canal – the first poetry trail of its kind. The statue was unveiled and MHPT launched on July 22nd 2023.

People have described my 'Myfanwy obsession' as a crusade, a mission, a calling, but however you describe it, I have felt compelled to put Myfanwy's work back in print. The fifty poems included in this book have been shaped by my conversations with the people I have met on my Myfanwy way. Each one carefully selected and featured under its rightful title, of which there are seven. The final chapter is made up of the twelve poems which feature on the new MHPT walks. Her poetry is brought to life for the first time in situ, from the Folly and the Grotto to the 'long liquid miles' of the Canal, as recited on the app by canal laureate Roy McFarlane.

Her first book *Fantasy*, followed by *Poems* and *More Poems*, all received great reviews from her older Welsh male contemporaries; Huw Menai, Will Ifan, and A.G. Prys, all observing that 'elfin lyricst' Myfanwy was a talented nature poet and 'the authentic wind, though it carries all the smoke of Pontypool in its arms.' Writing from the heart about the green lanes of Monmouthshire to the trampled grass of Kensington, Eliot Crawshay-Williams (Parliamentary Private Secretary to Lloyd George and Winston Churchill) praised her poetry acknowledging its wide appeal:

> We who are of Wales will rejoice that they have an intrinsically Cymric inspiration – incidentally, the beauty of Welsh place-names is recognised and used with effect; but they strike deeper than any merely local soil.

I was delighted to be commissioned by BBC Radio Wales to make an Arts documentary *My Hill of Dreams: The Story of Myfanwy Haycock*. It presented the opportunity for me to take Myfanwy's poetry to today's poets, scholars, historians, and journalists to gain a better understanding of where her place in poetry lies today. Poems such as 'Penance' and 'Before the Storm' speak of love, a topic I discussed with Art historian Peter Lord, who had first discovered Myfanwy whilst he was researching the painter, Maurice Sochachewsky for his book *Relationships with Pictures*. Maurice and Myfanwy started a relationship when he came to paint 'Real life underground' coalminers in Pontnewynydd in 1937. Peter is the custodian of some sixty letters written by Maurice to his mother speaking of his love for Myfanwy. Peter gave an invaluable insight in to why Myfanwy's career may not have been more widely remembered;

> After the Second Word War, Myfanwy's lyrical landscape poetry went drastically out of fashion, which is sad, because it's meant that her work has been lost for several generations. The things that's happening now, is that we are able to look at it with fresh eyes, having come through that period of modernism, and now being able to look at that as part of the history, we can look back with a clearer vision, and evaluate the work of Myfanwy in poetry.

Two world wars had started and finished by the time Myfanwy was twenty six. In her poem 'Red for Mourning', we hear Myfanwy's war time frustrations as she proclaims 'I'll rattle the stars together as I dance in my gown of red'. BBC Head of History, Robert Seatter, spoke with me about limited opportunities for women in the 1940-50's, giving an insight into the early days of BBC broadcasting in London, which being a Welsh woman with a Welsh accent, was an almighty challenge:

Many of the poets in the early decades were male. We struggled to find women, we struggled to find poets of colour, so that's why Myfanwy is an important voice because she's a woman voice, who appeared on the radio and she's also a Welsh voice, which is significant. Those three things are absolute reason for maintaining her legacy.

The *Western Mail* was pivotal to Myfanwy's journalistic career and to hear their first female editor, Catrin Pascoe, say that 'Myfanwy carved the way for women journalists like myself' is testament to why her work now needs to be remembered.

At the time of Myfanwy's death in 1963, she was compiling her poetry book *Mountain over Paddington* which was published posthumously, just months after she passed away. Myfanwy scholar and retired doctor, Godfrey Brangham, offered me some perspective on this sad time of her life, as reflected in her final poems 'Cuckoo' and 'Across My Dark'. He also shared with me a unique story based on a true account direct from sister Gwladys about the day that Dylan Thomas came and knocked on Myfanwy's door.

The reviews for *Mountain over Paddington* were bittersweet. Welsh writer Fred Hando wrote that W.H. Davies 'held her in high esteem; I am sure Islywn would have welcomed her as [a] daughter-poet; and for this reviewer no stanzas are more redolent of the Monmouthshire scene than "Caravans at dawn".'

Another review said;

Myfanwy Haycock has experienced many faces of life and she polished every one making her literary output shine like a diamond among broken glass. She had known something of the heart searing tragedy of war and soul sapping paths of illness, yet there was a unity of theme that ran through her poetry like a golden thread giving it a delicate tone and an appealing tenderness. Whether she was in her native land with all its childhood associations, climbing its mountains and hills of Monmouthshire, roaming the valleys and exploring rivers and smokey, foggy landscape, this talented poetess was able to visualise beauty in all she saw and sing a song with the cadence of a great organ. She could extract the sweetest music from the most indifferent score, clocking the back coal tips and scarred valleys of Wales with a raiment spun from the finest gold and refined in the heart that was forever Welsh.

Determined to continue her legacy, her sister Gwladys and son David Wynn published *Hill of Dreams, Some Perfect Morning*, and a collection of her Christmas poems *A Tale that is True*.

A.G. Prys-Jones wrote:

> Those who carry no chips on their shoulders, but accept with gratitude the daily grace and joy they find in the ordinary things of life are the true inheritors of the earth, never bored of frustrated despite the suicidal stupidities of our rootless, restless inquisitive society. Myfanwy Haycock certainly belonged to this company. She found grace and beauty everywhere, distilling her impressions in vivid word-pictures of charm and tenderness, her imagery, often touched with elfin whimsically is free and appealing. Fatally captive overlooking her rival garden and the rolling Surrey woodlands she could still write:

> 'Here in a world of songs and wings where times a shadow scare defines
> My tranquil heart can seek and find infinity in finite things.'

('This Way')

I was born twenty years after Myfanwy died and although we never met, we both originated from the same hometown of Pontypool. At the start of my research, there was a part of me that wondered 'Could this be the reason why I feel such a connection to her?' Now, after speaking to so many inspiring people, I have no doubt that there is a place for Myfanwy's poetry in 21st century Wales and beyond. I know it goes far deeper than our shared hometown. I believe that the recent trend for upcycling furniture extends into the poetic realm. There are so many contemporary poets with new rhymes and reasons. National Poet of Wales Hanan Issa recently read some of Myfanwy's poems – 'Fugitive' and 'Return' – at a special poetry evening I organised in Torfaen Museum. She said it was an honour to read Myfanwy's work; 'Make way for the moon and me.'

Peter Lord is correct in saying that 'Her work has been lost... until now.' And, so my Myfanwy secret is officially out. Her work is back in print for the sixtieth anniversary year. Her sculpture, a tangible reminder of a female poet, now sits in Pontypool Park and people are once again walking her hill of dreams! As a lifelong reader and believer in the work of Myfanwy Haycock, I feel that in some small way, I have directed her into the hands of you, the reader, and for that I can only hope that Myfanwy is, as I know I am, 'laughing up my sleeve'.

Jenni Crane

FROM

Fantasy
(1937)

Fantasy

Last night I caught a moon, sickle and silver,
And hung it in the shadows of my hair,
I stayed awhile among the lilies, hoping
    That Pierrot would come there.
I made a wreath of dreams, shell-dreams and wonders,
Set thick with jewels of a lovely day;
I sang a young, young roundelay of birdsong,
    But Pierrot stayed away!

To-night I'll throw the lily-heads, all bleeding,
Into the burning of a golden moon,
And hear the wind in torn, sad stems a-sobbing
    That 'Pierrot will come soon.'
To-night I'll tie the peacocks' tails in tangles,
To-night I'll sing a different kind of song,
To-night, when thoughts are red and dreams are shattered,
    Pierrot will come along!

Disillusion

I had planned
to sing you a song,
If only a bird would begin it;
A dream-misty song, a windy-wild song,
With twilight and star-music in it.

I had planned
To give you a dream
That only a poet could fashion;
An old-golden dream, a warm, Autumn dream,
Aglow with chrysanthemum passion.

I had planned
To give you the moon,
If only a tree-top would hold it;
A full-blown moon, oh! a maddening moon,
And a star-scorched cloud to enfold it.

I had planned
To give you my love,
If only I thought you would take it;
My will-o'-wisp love, my young, eager love,
And my heart – though I knew you would break it.

I had planned
To give you a song and a dream and my love,
And the moon to hold in your hand,
But suddenly, suddenly I knew
You would never understand.

The Madman

Black witches chased him through his night-filled world;
He fled before them, knew not that he had fled;
And all around him roaring giants hurled
Great stars to kill him, knowing he had sinned;
And still before him as he onward sped
    The Great Moon grinned.

O God, that moon, it would not hide its face,
That moon, that moon with round, eternal stare!
It rolled before him in his frenzied race,
He could not lose it, could not veil his sight!
Great moon-faced moths were tangled in his hair,
    That moon-filled night.

And then he thought 'what if the moon were dead?'
And tried to smash it on a velvet hill,
Then peeped with dawning hope – the moon still led!
He screamed with rage and tore a passing wind,
He hurled a stone – in awe the stars stood still –
    The Great Moon grinned!

Hot witch-breath licked his neck, long brambles caught
His waving arms and tore his clammy skin;
He sought for something, knew not what he sought.
Hot, pointed stars were dancing in his head;
He knew the moon was mad – oh God, that grin!
    The moon still led.

Black witches chased him down a country lane,
A honeysuckle lane where water shone;
He stopped his flight – the witches hastened on.
He saw a pale moon in a pool of rain,
And knew that he had sought and he had found.
Glad, frothy chuckles stirred the sleeping day,
He fell upon his knees and tried to pray –
The moon was dead,
    The Grinning Moon was drowned!

The Bird

Last night a bird sang, somewhere in a wood;
Sudden and clear its raptures cleft the night;
The moon, entangled in the bird's delight,
Listened awhile and knew that it was good.
    Last night a bird sang, somewhere in a wood.

Its golden bill was all adrip with song;
Singing, it mocked the silence with its mirth;
Shattered the silence of a sleeping Earth!
The leaves, moon-soaked and heavy, gently stirred,
Loving the pagan singing of the bird
    Whose golden bill was all adrip with song.

Around the still, star-smothered night there rang
The daring challenge of the joy-filled bird –
But nothing answered, though the night had heard!
Into the Past Beyond the echoes rang;
    I wonder why it sang?

July

Above this hill the smooth white clouds drift on
Like listless flocks a-weary with the heat,
And cast their shadows down like giant feet
    That step from hill to hill, and then are gone.

Far in the valley where the heat haze lies,
And roads are whiter than a wood dove's wings,
Usk swirls 'neath Kemys bridge and gently sings
    Of cool wet blueness caught from summer skies.

Softly the river's liquid lullaby
Lilts through the shallows, and where pools are deep
It croons to old Llancayo, drowsed with sleep,
    Of all the golden magic of July.

July, and sleep, and green enchanted dreams
Of sun-splashed lanes and poppy-threaded hay,
Of drunken bees that tumble from the spray,
    And dragonflies a-dance on dancing streams.

July in Monmouthshire – the clouds drift by,
The shadows slowly move; the swallows cry,
The ruined mill is blurred against the sky.
            It is July!

The Taskmaster

You do not understand; your hand was given
A mystic power to fashion lovely things,
And yet I know your heart is never riven
With pain and beauty when a blackbird sings.

I am all dreams, my heart, my soul, my being!
You do not know, you cannot understand;
You stay awhile and watch me, only seeing
My fumbling fingers and unsteady hand.

You do not understand my love of dreaming,
For you have never dreamed; you cannot see
The wonder of a bird with white wings gleaming,
The breathless beauty of a wind-swept tree!

You have a power.   If only I could take it
Away from all the emptiness of you,
I would enslave it, mould and bend and break it,
To serve my dreams, until they all came true!

FROM

Poems
(1944)

Red For Mourning

I will wear red for mourning,
  I will ring bells for tears,
I will draw passionate music
  From the discordant years;

I will wear red for mourning,
  I'll dance with the marionettes,
Treading on toes of shadows,
  Buffeting pale regrets;

I will wear red for mourning,
  My candles shall all be lit,
And only one bird on the hedgerow
  Shall fathom the cause of it;

And I'll tie his tongue with a cobweb,
  Lest he should sing my pain,
Then I'll light yet another candle
  And ring all the bells again;

And I'll rattle the stars together
  As I dance in my gown of red –
I will wear red for mourning
  Because of a dream that is dead.

Penance

I am knitting a garment of sound
From the woollen noise of your voice:
In – 'round – through and around –
Every stitch is a word
I have heard
Or not heard.
Time withers while I knit;
It seems there can be no end to it.

See how the pattern goes!
Plain platitudes, grey wool;
Soon it will reach my toes,
Soon it will be a shroud
Of words both loud
And not loud.
With woollen words I knit –
It seems there can be no end to it.

Longer it grows and grows,
Now I am muffled in words,
Your words in unvaried rows
Looped on unflinching pins;
To atone for my sins
Or your sins,
I knit and knit and knit –
The start was the only end to it!

The Little Man

His nose is a roof-gutter where sound runs
slim as a pin;
He could never utter words like guns
rolling within
Down to his fingers and his toes
like thunder.
His slow sound lingers on his nose
then drops under
His stubbly grey chin. It cannot be found!
was it there?
Give him a safety-pin to pin his sound
to his hair.

His voice is a trickle somewhere and nowhere
of pale sound;
Each word a tickle like dust or a hair
blowing around;
There is no kindness in it, no note that's gay,
and no sorrow –
Pale sound each minute, yesterday, today,
and tomorrow.
Yet somewhere I've heard that though he's surly
and his voice slim,
There's a certain blackbird gets up early
to sing to him.

Solitude

The green gate creaks – did anyone come in?
  And what was that? Did anybody knock?
There's so much noise, the kettle's pompous din,
  The shrill, incessant teasing of the clock.

A distant train goes coughing up the hill,
  Crisp leaves drift loudly in the flower-bed.
And in the churchyard where all should be still,
  A noisy blackbird serenades the dead.

There's such a noise! The very tap-drips talk
  In rumbling basses, and the glint-eyed cat
Who should have paws of thistledown, now stalks
  On paws of granite to her corner mat.

Oh, such a noise! Both outside and within,
  The greying embers roar and break apart,
Then comes the thunder of a falling pin
  Made louder by the silence of my heart.

Noise

My feet made all the noise in Kensington;
  Sunday was fast asleep, the houses lay
Sleepily arm-in-arm and almost snored;
  My feet went thundering on and would not stay.

I drowned my ears in thought to drown the noise
  Of feet that rang like tempests in the street;
My feet made all the noise in Kensington –
  I grew afraid because of thundering feet.

But on and on they went, as loud as winds,
  As loud as mountains walking side-by-side,
Louder than sudden laughter in a church,
  Or silence in a room where someone died.

And so, ashamed, I urged them to the park,
  Indolent park on Sunday holiday,
And there my feet went thundering down the walks
  With roar that swept all other sound away.

So flaming anger drove me under trees,
  Across green lawns I made my loud feet pass;
Then, God be praised! their thundering grew still –
  But oh! the shouting of the trampled grass!

In the Garden

The gramophone three doors away
  Cuts the white sunshine into strips
With blades of music; tulips sway
  Large-headed from their slim green hips.

The deck-chair's caterpillar stripes
  Merge with the music, blue and red,
While by the gate laburnum drips
  Gold tears upon the border bed.

A swallow skims between the notes –
  A blue-black moment slipping by –
And on that last arpeggio
  There rides a yellow butterfly.

Oh, painted, burnished afternoon!
  Must your bewildering colours fade
Deep into all the Yesterdays
  That all the years have ever made?

Could I but turn those fleeting notes
  And head them round the other way,
I'd pour all Springtime back into
  The gramophone three doors away!

FROM

More Poems
(1945)

Black-out

The stars have never, never seemed so bright,
Nor earth so grimly black; there are no fields,
No gates, no glowing lamps; just stars and height.

There are no people, only stumbling sounds
Along the blackness where the road once was.
This strange and Stygian darkness knows no bounds
Of length or breadth save where the stars begin;
A desolate dog outside an unseen house
Wails bleakly like an ill-tuned violin.

A little wind gropes blindly up the street
Along the chasms where the gutters were,
And shuffles paper-scraps with cautious feet.

Two stars have fallen from the Milky Way,
And Puss, aloft on an invisible wall,
Has caught them in her eyes. The tall trees sway
Blackly against the star-bespattered sky,
Shaking their drying leaves in shadowed waves
Of ebony rhythm and black harmony.

There is no length, no breadth, no ray of light
In all this shapeless, night-witched world, but oh
The stars, the stars have never been so bright!

Return

I've come back from Wales
   And I've carried with me
Speech that runs warm
   In my memory;
A vision of hills
   And a straggling town,
And roads that toil up
   When they ought to run down.

A tree wild with wind
   Like a billowing ship,
And scavenging sheep
   On a black coal-tip;
A silhouette of pit-wheels
   That spin overhead,
Like spiders caught close
   In their own cunning thread.

Yes, I've come back from Wales
   And I've brought all the way
Treasures to please me
   For many a day,
Treasures to cherish
   Yet Oh! Now I find
I've brought all these things
   But my heart's left behind.

Dying Flame

This candle of my love is burning dim;
Soon, soon its flame must die,
And dance no more, resilient, golden, slim,
Leaning to breath of laughter or of sigh,
Challenging all the wildest winds that blow –
My candle's burning very, very low.

This faithful petal-flame, this thread of fire
Has danced and fluttered to my heart's desire,
Has drunk the tears of love in long, hot sips,
And kissed the breasts of love with golden lips;
Yet now I watch its lovely glory fade –
My flame is dying and I am afraid.

There's so much still to burn, the wick is trim,
Yet every moment sees the flame grow dim;
Not long ago it dared the tempest's wrath,
And leaped and danced to hear the wind-gods shout,
So brave and strong it seemed – yet now a moth
May shake its wings and put my candle out.

Fugitive

I am tired of walking alone;
Let the moon come down and walk with me,
Let him trundle his portly, cumbersome form at my side.
See, the street is so wide!
There is room for the moon to walk with me –
But no room for me to hide.

Yes, let the moon come down.
I will watch his crescent profile and he
Will walk unconcerned in his own flat, nebulous glow;
Unwavering he will throw
A long smooth glance in front and then I will see
There is nowhere for me to go.

Perhaps he will look at me,
But I know there will be no speech for us;
I cannot talk to moons for I'm not yet dead.
But his fat glow will spread
On and still on, and I'll need no words to know
The blackness that lies ahead.

Make way for the moon and me!
Make way for us in the tunnel of streets!
He shows me as surely as words that there is no crack
In the infinite wall of black.
I know there is nowhere, nowhere for me to go –
And I cannot turn back.

Standing Room Only

Pools swallow rain like swords,
Dead leaves lie passive on grit
As on beds of nails;
Trees like skeleton-men
Posture on pavements,
And soon that corner house
With a turret like a turban
Will be doing the rope trick.

There is dangerous silence
In the over-crowded ninepenny gallery
High up in my brain;
Soon booings and catcalls
Will spill into the auditorium,
For it seems that only I, who am greater
And so much less than those buskers,
Cannot swallow swords, lie on nails,
Dare not go naked in the streets,
And will never do the rope trick.

To a Critic

I did not understand – until you told me –
   That flowers are 'merely flowers' and trees 'just trees'
That wind and rain and sunshine only hold me
   In 'superficial, empty' ecstasies.

I did not understand – until you said it –
   That love and laughter, too, are 'out of date,'
Nor did I blast all Nature with discredit
   Until you voiced your subtle hymn of hate.

I did not realise that 'times have altered,'
   That green and lovely things have 'had their day,'
But now I know why all my songs have faltered,
   And all my dreams have fallen by the way!

I did not think to write of smoke-filled hours,
   Of turmoil, torture, murder, ruin, rape,
Nor had I thought my songs of birds and flowers
   Were but a 'weak and cowardly escape.'

But now I understand – since you've informed me –
   And for my foolish past I humbly grieve –
But while you're smugly thinking you've reformed me,
   I'm laughing, laughing, laughing up my sleeve!

FROM

Mountain over Paddington
(1964)

At the Concert

The violinist peeled thin notes like rind
From silver apples of sound,
Flinging them down before him and behind,
Beating them to the ground,
While the rich cellos and deep double-basses
Stayed dumb and awestruck in their second places.

Piano, harp and clarinet were still;
Only the shrill, provocative violin
Gave forth bewildering melody until
It seemed we must begin
To laugh or weep or dance! How could we sit
While someone played a tune with stars in it?

We should have danced out into city streets,
Or wept until the whole world's tears were shed,
Or laughed until we tumbled from our seats
In ecstasy; instead
With condescending hum and gallery cheers
We primly praised that music of the spheres.

To Greet My Love

Love, I'll tell the streets of London
That you are coming to town,
Coming from the heart of Wales;
I'll sleek my hair like ebony
And wear a scarlet gown,
Scarlet as the lacquer on my nails.
Like a flame I'll sear through London
To meet you when you come,
My thoughts will fly before me
Like a million bees a-hum,
Oh! my heart will beat, will beat, will beat
Just like a frenzied drum,
To greet my love who comes from Wales.

I'll flash across the London parks
And tell the trees and grass
That my love is coming up to town,
All the taxi-cabs and buses
Will start dancing as I pass,
Flaming in my scarlet gown.
The very tallest buildings
Will curtsey, bob and sway,
And the smallest ones will giggle
As I speed upon my way
To greet my love, my love from Wales
Who says he comes to stay –
Oh! my love is coming up to town.

Love, I'll tell the streets of London
That I love you more than all,
Lover from the heart of Wales
I see you like a mountain, love,
So beautiful and tall,
Plynlimon when the dawning pales.

Yes, a mountain over Paddington
My splendid love will be,
Like the water-songs of Dovey
His greeting words to me,
And he'll hold the scarlet flame of me
For all the world to see –
My lovely love who comes from Wales!

Flower-Shop Window

You seem so conscious of your elegance,
You haughty tulip, regal daffodil!
Almost you stare amazed to see me rest
My shopping-basket on your window-sill.

And that rich rose, I'm sure I saw her nudge
A pink carnation, doubtless hoping I –
That laden, windswept gipsy through the pane –
Would never dare to step inside and buy!

You out-of-season lilies, orchids rare,
You smug anemones, though I admit
Your perfect loveliness, to-day I find
No happiness in contemplating it.

For this untidy, gipsy self of me
Sees shy, wild daffodils all cool with rain
In some deep wood at home, and oh, my heart
Aches for white violets in a country lane!

Tell Me

Tell me, is there snow at home,
And do my lovely mountains lie
Like great white fallen angels there
Beneath a numb and sorrowing sky?
And is there winter in the woods
Where nothing, nothing, seems to live?
And have you sensed the quietness
That only trees and snow can give?

Have drips and drops of water turned
To long glass fingers overnight?
And, closely pressed against the wall,
Is one frail jasmine star alight?
Do starlings scream upon the roof,
And does the chubby robin wait
Upon the sill, just like a bright
Red apple on a cold white plate?

Do tomtits swing, pale blue and gold,
Upon the bare forsythia branch?
Do clouds with kindly fingers stroke
The furrowed forehead of Pentranch?
And have the hungry sheep come down
From mountain tracks, and do they roam
Like timid ghosts around the town?
Tell me, is there snow at home?

This Way

I look out over Surrey now,
Content that it should be this way,
Nor miss my mountains tall and grey,
Here where the highest hills are low.

Like galleons with golden sails
I watch the slow sweet days drift by,
Patterned against the Autumn sky,
Drifting towards the West – and Wales.

Here in a world of songs and wings
Where Time's a shadow scarce defined,
My tranquil heart can seek and find
Infinity in finite things.

And all I ask is just to stay
Quiet and hear the grasses grow
In these soft Surrey meadows now,
Content that it should be this way.

Cuckoo

Each day the cuckoo sings as if
  His song were new and rare,
As if before such melody
  Had never filled the air.

Lest we should fail to hear his lay
  He sings it o'er and o'er,
And dares us from his heart to say
  We've heard that tune before!

And we who waste so many words
  Nor heed their precious worth,
Why should we grudge his simple pride
  Or mock his merry mirth?

Though we may have the gift of tongues,
  Hold magic in our throats,
He captures all of summer
  In two lovely foolish notes!

FROM

Hill of Dreams

(1988)

Cardiff

Day – and the throb of traffic,
The ceaseless whirr of cars;
Night – and slenderly-stencilled spires
Tipped with spindle stars;
Ships and shops and avenues in a city by the sea –
These are but few of the coloured thoughts
    That Cardiff gives to me.

Lawn-encircled castle
    Of Neo-Gothic art,
Palaces and peacocks
    In a crowded city's heart;
The hustle and the bustle of countless busy feet;
And Springtime flower sellers
    Along St. Mary Street.

Gleaming civic buildings,
    Pillars, domes and towers,
A golden clock with golden voice
    To sing of civic hours.
Stately trees that murmur, tall and greenly dark,
And march in slow procession
    Around a sleepy park.

The shining stare of windows
    In wonder-shops that hold
Furs and gowns and laces,
    And bales of cloth-of-gold.
Clanging trams that hurtle along a sunny street,
And coffee's warm aroma
    Where morning gossips meet.

Magic roads to Dockland –
    To France or far Japan –
Gay with the carefree lure of things
    Cosmopolitan;

Sad with a quiet sadness that will not drift away,
Where the spirit of the Orient breathes
    In the heart of Tiger Bay.

All this, all this in Cardiff –
    The ceaseless whir of cars,
A tiny brown-thatched cottage,
    And spires tipped with stars;
And splashed and tangled in the dreams that Cardiff gives to me,
Are ships and shops and Beauty
    In a City by the sea.

Llangorse

When the hills were pale with morning and woods were half-awake,
I found a fairy village by a lovely fairy lake.

Oh! the witchery and whiteness of each sun-splashed cottage wall,
The friendly slant of slated roofs where chimney shadows fall.

There were scarlet apples hanging from strangely twisted trees,
And golden pears were swinging very softly in the breeze.

Oh! the daring, flaring riot of flowers every-where,
Geraniums and marigolds and clematis were there;

There were hedges laced with gossamer, and butterflies flew high
Where honeysuckle bugles were calling to the sky.

Oh! the dreamy, dreamy silence as though nothing were awake
Where grey Llangasty Church kept watch across the sleeping lake.

And the little hills were giants, by sudden glory kissed,
For all the mighty Beacons had vanished in the mist –

There was magic in the morning, silver woods were half awake,
And I found a fairy village by a lovely fairy lake.

Llancayo Mill

Beyond the tufty-fingered hedge,
Across the misty meadow,
The old mill rises in a wedge
Of silver shadow.
*
Like some old woman dozing there
Beside the drowsy river,
With straggling straw-threads in her hair,
And bones a-shiver,
She mumbles grumbles with a frown
At every drifting year –
Hush! With a rush there clatters down
A stony tear.

She hears no more the taunting howls
Of twisted windy laughter,
Nor heeds the haunting hoots of owls
From crumbling rafter;

And while she dumbly, glumly grieves
That she is grey and old,
Her thick green shawl of ivy-leaves
Keeps out the cold.

She sits where she has always sat,
And though her head is bent,
She wears a sea-gull on her hat
As ornament;
Her moss-patched skirt is faded brown,
Her dull eyes dimly peer –
Hush! With a rush there clatters down
Another tear!
*
Across the fields the old, old mill,
With sleepy, senile wits,
Through summer's heat and winter's chill
Just sits and sits and sits.

At Llanover

I have forgotten all towns;
I can only recall
A slow, brown path that tiptoed under the trees,
A blackbird's song and grass on an old stone wall –
I can only remember these.

For that slow brown path from nowhere
Has led at last
Into this unassuming Arcady
Where there's only Present, no Future or even a Past,
For a moment's Eternity.

And my world goes just to the tops
Of the distant hills;
There is no beyond, no torture of infinite space;
And the wind comes soft where the first wild daffodils
Are lit in this quiet place.

There is no more ceaseless rattle
Of trains and cars,
No blatant buildings, elbowing, ugly and strong,
But cottages whose windows shine like stars,
And a stream that is full of song.

I have forgotten all towns;
I can only recall
A slow, brown path that tiptoed under the trees,
A blackbird's song and grass on an old stone wall –
I shall always remember these.

On the Mountain Road near Blaenavon

I feel that I have been this way before,
Along the narrow way that straggles o'er
The hill's brown shoulder.
Each grey and patient boulder,
Each twisted branch on every wind-torn tree,
Has waked elusive memories in me.

These things are so familiar-sweet, the sun
All amber-gold, the startled sheep that run
Among the heather.
That gay coquettish feather
Of drifting cloud, these gutter-gurgling streams –
They stir to life half-haunting, taunting dreams.

The road is like a living thing. It leaps
Across the mountainside's soft folds, and creeps
Within the hollows,
Then suddenly it follows
Obediently the old stone wall that throws
A friend's arm around it as it goes

Upon its downward way. It will not wait
For someone to unlatch the mountain gate;
But slips below it,
Half turning then to blow it
A pebbly kiss – Oh I am very sure
That I have walked along this road before!

Those purple patches where the sun has kissed
The withered heather's faded amethyst,
The wind that flutters
Across the grass, and mutters
Impatiently around the mountain's crest –
These things have filled my heart with strange unrest.

Should I remember when I came this way,
And why elusive memories today
Have haunted me
And mocked and taunted me,
Should I remember – I might hold the key
That opens the incomprehensive door
To Life and Death and All Eternity –

I know that I have been this way before.

Raglan Castle

I saw it first when Spring had softly kissed
With faery splendour those old walls, and when
The towers rose clear-cut, etched in amethyst
Against the sky's cold, rain-washed blueness. Then
I came again this way on longer days
When trees were darkly green, and Summer lay
Bemused and misty in a quiet haze
That dimmed those tranquil towers to distant grey.

Now it is Autumn. Trees and towers unite
In golden harmony; the great walls glow
With cinnamon, primrose, peach and russet light.
When Winter comes I'll pass this way again;
Earth will be black and silver, and I know
My heart will break – will break with beauty – then.

FROM

Some Perfect Morning
(1991)

Some Perfect Morning

Is all my singing done then?
  Is ecstasy all found?
Have last dry notes been drained then
  From sediment of sound?
Is there no song in stillness
  In quietude no theme?
Is fantasy a phantom
  Of some half-faded dream?
Can I not snatch some rhythm
  From this neat march of years,
Nor strike one silver couplet
  From thin white glass of tears?
Or are my songs all sung then,
  And ecstasy all found
And last numb dumb notes wrung then
  From sediment of sound?
Nay, ere you set those sad bells
  For my dead raptures ringing,
Know that some perfect morning
  I will awaken singing!

Returning

The bluebells all had bloomed and gone,
Young grass had lengthened to hay,
The rain had come, the sun had shone
Though I was far away.

Yet it had seemed that when I went
The trees and flowers must die of grief,
The stream lose all its melody,
The hedges lose each leaf!

When I came back my heart grew sad
And hot my tears were burning
Though every tree and flower seemed glad
To welcome my returning –

For though soft beech leaves stroked my hair
And foxgloves stood tiptoe and kissed me,
I knew that though they seemed to care
They never really missed me!

Before the Storm

There is no music in the pinewood now,
No songs half-way to Heaven – all is still;
And slow, black thunder-clouds are creeping low
    Above the hill.

Only the distant, desolate cries of sheep
Stir thinly through the thick lethargic air;
Twilight has come too soon, and warm, drugged sleep
    Is everywhere.

Against the hedge proud foxgloves taper high,
And steep their purple splendour in a glow
Of angry amber captured from the sky;
    All in a row,

Six ducklings waddle sadly from the stream,
Moon daisies stare in pale faced apathy
At one another, then more palely still
    They stare at me.

There is no wind, no vacant breeze to snap
Cool fingers at the sun. Heart, mute your beat,
Lest your least throb should seem a thunder-clap!
    The board, flat heat

Is wedged 'twixt earth and heaven; languidly
The Sugar Loaf leans darkly on the sky
Where sullen clouds assemble silently,
    There is no cry

Of bird or beast save those bewildering cries,
A million miles away, of desolate sheep.
Beyond the wood a shy, brown village lies,
    Half watchful, half asleep.

The mute, inscrutable earth is very still;
No note of music falls from any tree.
Thunder is brooding low upon the hill –
    And in the heart of me.

—

September Song

The Grandad of Apple Trees just can't remember
In all his long history, right back to Eve,
A windier, wetter and wilder September –
Or so all of you little red apples believe,
You must be so weary of soggy green grasses,
Of sullen limp raindrops and querulous sky,
Of sudden leaves clinging in cumbersome masses,
And blackbirds too gloomy to whistle or fly.

But see! Tufts of sunlight like wakening flowers –
Bright tasselled chrysanthemums yellow as bees –
Are threaded on thin silver ribbons of showers
And tangled all over the wet apple trees.
And the Grandad of Apple Trees, there by the gateway,
Creaks his gnarled knuckles and winks at the sun,
In an orchard grown crazy with blackbirds, and straightway
A sun-sifted pattern of song is begun.

So dry all those tears now, little red apples,
And wipe with green fingers your smooth rosy cheeks,
For sunshine steams warmly through wetness and dapples
A world where it's surely been raining for weeks!

Butterfly in a Garage

Just like a wisp of snow on a sullen day
You drifted idly through the greasy gloom,
Seeking in your remote, meandering way
In that unlikely place some fragrant bloom.

You quivered past the unresponsive lathe,
Skimmed briefly over petrol-scummy pools,
Then hovered like an absent-minded wraith
Above square-shouldered cans and oily tools.

Then suddenly amid the cars you flew
Wildly, all panic-stricken now to be
Trapped without sunshine, flower-scent or dew
In that dark world of mute machinery.

Strange contrast this! Your fragile beauty gleamed
Against strong cars, those arrogant, swift things –
Yet how uncouth and cumbersome they seemed
Beside the frail perfection of your wings!

Across My Dark

I wish, Lord, I believed in You!
My faith's a frail and transient thing,
Enriched and bold in Beauty's glow,
Yet swiftly sped on Sorrow's wing.

For life and light I offer praise,
My heart is quick to bless Your Name,
Yet in the sad and fearful ways
I cannot trust in You the same.

A strange God this, Who only guides
Through pleasant paths and ways of peace,
And strange this heart that faints and hides
When shadows fall and pleasures cease.

I stretch my doubting hand to Him
Across my dark, yet fail to sense
Down pathways growing chill and dim,
The glory of His innocence.

Maybe there'll come some perfect hour
When hand meets hand in close accord,
Then night will blossom like a flower,
And in the dark I'll praise my Lord.

FROM

A Tale That Is True
(1992)

Christmas Tree

Now in your crisp green hands you hold
Slim candles tipped with wisps of gold,
And like a diadem you wear
A trembling star upon your hair.
What are you dreaming, little tree?
Is your wild spirit glad to be
All tinsel-tangled, spun with snow,
And gilded by the fire's deep glow?

'Outside there's strange rich mystery
And, wonder,' said the Christmas Tree,
'While high above my dear lost hill
A Holy Star shines, pure and chill'
But by the fireside, little tree,
There's much to hear and much to see,
Laughter, joy and quick surprise
Like Christmas stars in children's eyes.

'Out on my dear lost hill I'd hear
A Seraph singing strong and clear,
And if I watched perhaps I'd see
Tall angels', said the Christmas tree;
'And oh! who knows, but waiting there
With flowers of frost upon my hair,
Thin Christmas, child I well might see.
Climbing my hill – to Calvary'.

He Came

There was no pageantry to mark His coming
No pomp to welcome His nativity,
Just one new Star 'mid all the stars of heaven,
For some to see.

There were no cheering crowds, no earthly choirs,
No bells to shake the cold air, shrill and clear;
Just strange glad angel songs, remote and mystic,
For some to hear.

Young Love was born with only two to love Him,
Sweet gentle Mary, weak and travel-worn,
And Joseph, grateful for a sheltering stable
On Christmas morn.

There were no tears of joy, no sighs of rapture,
And only Mary whispered His dear name –
And yet our hearts are all a little kinder
Because He came.

FROM

The Myfanwy Haycock Poetry Trail
(2023)

Hiking

I love to walk
Where little roads are winding up and down;
But long and dusty is the broad highway
That leads to Monmouth town;
So, I will go
Where narrow fairy byroads dip and rise,
And walk to sunset from the dawn of day
Just as the black crow flies.

I love to walk
Where silver birches drop their lacy veils
And hide their feet in beds of tender grass
In Monmouth's lovely dales.
'Tis good to know
That Beauty ever keeps an open door,
To know that I can leave things as I pass
As lovely as before.

I love to walk
Along a winding lane where banks are high,
With walls of youngling oaks on either side
Arched by eternal sky.
I love to pass
Where winds are keen and heather perfumes blow,
Where tiny violets open blue eyes wide,
Where little sheep-tracks go.

And if there's one
Who only finds a God in man-made things,
Who hears, but only dimly understands
The prayer a wild bird sings,
Who only knows
The empty joy of unenlightened talk –
If he would wander into faery land,
Then let him walk.

Fragment

What shall I leave you when I go a-journeying,
What shall I leave you when I go my way
Ten tall poplar trees
Like long green fingers,
And a fine day.

Ten tall poplar trees, a day of fine weather,
Burnished blackberries shining in the sun,
Ducklings waddling
Sedately in the farmyard,
One by one.

What shall I leave you? Blackberries and ducklings,
Snow piled high and clean along a country lane,
Thin winds wailing
In telegraph wires,
And spots of rain.

These I will leave you, that you may remember,
And hear my songs in wind and rain when I go my way,
And see my dreams in blackberries,
Trees and snow and ducklings,
And a fine day.

The Hill of Dreams

There is a hill
Enriched with poppy-glory and a-gleam
With drifting veils of moondust, petal-edged,
For one who dreams a dream.
A hill of dreams, where men may bring their treasure,
Crushed star dreams, misty day dreams wrought in vain;
And, waking, fill again the emptied measure,
With thoughts of new dreams – old dreams born again.

There is a hill
Where timid dream-sheep linger, and where hide,
Among the lily flowers, shy, peeping things –
The ghosts of dreams that died!
And where tall tree-gods press against the heavens
Their clear defined and black entangled bars,
There is a little pool of soft dream water
Where float a million stars.

There is a hill
Where wine-red poppies droop and lost winds weep;
Where weary men may lay their burdens down,
And tired dreams may sleep.
A hill of dreams! but who may reach its summit,
And stand where jewelled rays of glory fall!
The One with Hidden Face, who cometh bearing
The greatest Dream of all!
*
Loud silence falls
Upon the little noises of the hill,
And 'midst the heavy heads of lily flowers
The ghosts of dreams are still.
The long black shadow of a rugged dream-Cross
Falls slantingly across the climbing ground
And in the darkened reaches of the water,
A million stars are drowned!

Mist in the Park

To-night the Round Pond is no longer round,
But just a limp light shadow on the mist
As though within itself it has been drowned.
Each sudden tree is like a threatening fist,
Knuckled and grimy, clenched towards the sky
That's muffled-up in sweaty woollen mist.

Oh quiet quietude! No breath or sigh
Stains the grey stillness with a smear of sound
Where no-one calls or comes: yet suddenly
In this lost place where only mists abound
I swear I saw a strange bright man go by,
And never once his swift feet touched the ground!

The Grotto, Pontypool

What artist soul conceived this fantasy
Of wild witch-beauty on a windy hill?
What patient fingers worked in harmony
With clouds and slender trees? What mystic skill
Patterned this floor with yellowed ivory,
And raised these walls of rough, unchiselled stones
And purple shadows? What strange imagery
Drew latent loveliness from shells and bones
And wove them into forms of mystery?
Who strove with mute, indomitable will,
And Beauty's pain-bewildered ecstasy,
To build this grotto on a windy hill?

'Tis only grass and trees and winds may sing
Of him whose hands achieved its fashioning.

The Folly, Pontypool

Here where the hill holds heaven in her hands,
High above Monmouthshire the grey tower stands.

He is weather-worn and scarred, and very wise,
For rainbows, clouds and stars shine through his eyes.

He was young for a hundred years, now he is old,
And his bones of stone rattle and crack with cold.

He who was proud and strong now shelters sheep;
He is weather-worn and scarred and full of sleep;

And he stares at space with a grave, octagonal frown,
While winds tear and tug at his crumbling crown.

He who is intimate with the ways of the moon,
And has known sun-ecstasy on a summer noon,

Now gives his dreams to the earth and the sky to keep –
He is weather-worn and scarred and kind to sheep;

And he wraps his head in mist lest he should see
The pathos of his own senility.

June Thoughts

There are green lanes in Monmouthshire, green lanes and pleasant ways
Across the curving hilltops and over shining streams,
And to those quiet places, on breathless summer days,
My vagrant heart goes stealing with the loveliest of dreams.

My vagrant heart goes stealing, on such a day as this,
Through haunted paths of Wentwood, all shadowy and still,
Where Usk is gently sighing 'neath the flooding tide's full kiss,
And little tracks are tangled 'midst the trees on Kemys Hill.

There are board fields in Monmouthshire, all silver-flecked with grain,
And great moon daises glowing through the honey perfumed hay;
And deep into the peace that dims a twilight-purple lane
My gipsy heart goes stealing on a June-enchanted day.

Cloud shadows on the Sugar Loaf, the song a river sings
When touched by rain's soft fingers tips, those sudden, mellow gleams
Of Sunlight on old Skirrid – these are the magic things
That I have stored within my heart and woven into dreams.

I know the lanes of Monmouthshire are shadowy and still,
And Usk is softly sighing 'neath the flooding tide's full kiss,
And oh! I know the broom is bright on every curving hill –
For my heart goes home to Monmouthshire, on such a day as this!

The Canal near Pontypool

Long, liquid miles
That bend and twist and creep
Darkly and imperturbably
Along,
Shallowly silver,
Bewilderingly deep,
Like a slow, green song.

The old canal –
Where sudden noises plop!
And then have never been,
And where
Twisting and twining's
Never seem to stop –
There's magic there;
Dragonfly magic
And gay forget-me-nots,
And strange rat-rustlings
In hidden holes,
While glassy water glints
Suddenly on dark dots
That are tadpoles.

Around the hills,
The little hills and ridges,
Mazed with meandering, it goes.
And swirls
Back on its tracks,
Threading its bridges
Like grey pearls.
Porcelain swans
On weed-green water glide
Inscrutably along,
While slender trees
Talk, talk incessantly
To trees on the other side.

The fat brown bees
Are grumbling
In a warm brown monotone
Among the meadowsweet and mint.
The grass
Leans water-wards,
Flower-tangled and wind-blown,
To see eels pass,
Sinuously.
The captive towpath trudges
Acquiescently between
Water and trees.
A swallow lightly skims
The waterway, and smudges
Reflections of trees.

Long, liquid miles
That bend and twist and creep
Darkly and imperturbably
Along,
Shallowly silver,
Bewilderingly deep,
Like a slow, green song.

Reflections

Deep in the river
   Clouds sail by,
And cows stand cool
   In liquid sky.

Tall tree-trunks taper
   Far below,
Their green leaves lift
   When breezes blow.

Oh, what a world
   Is here begun,
Where sky and water
   Are as one;

Where swallows skim
   The river bed –
Lord, am I standing
   On my head? –

Where fishes swim
   In cloud-splashed sky
And dodge those swallows
   Skimming by;

Where weeds and stones
   And treetops crowd,
And brown cows drink
   Great draughts of cloud;

Where winds shake trees
   Without a sound –
Lord, am I here,
   Or am I drowned?

Washing Day

It's washing day in Monmouthshire;
Along the swirly-whirly streams
The celandines have lit a fire,
It seems, it seems.

That every valley is a tub,
A 'foam with apple-blossom suds,
Where wind and rain and sunshine scrub
The new, fat buds

Of oaks and elms and sycamores,
With gurgles, giggles, grunts and groans
The brooks have scoured their pebbly floors
Like clean, white bones.

Half-glimpsed through tattered water-shrouds,
Across the blue, high-arching sky
Are rows and rows of puffy clouds
Hung up to dry.

Upon the hill the little house
In fine new whitewash sits and stares
Bright-eyed, like a bewildered mouse.
The hawthorn wears

A crisp new coat of green; the lane
That hops downhill and leaps the streams
Is splashed with primroses and rain.
It seems, it seems

That every valley's full of foam
Of steam and sunshine, froth and fire –
It's windy washing day at home
In Monmouthshire!

The Miner's Garden

Whenever time can set him free,
From labyrinthine burrowings,
From pin-point lights, black darkness and
Monotonous meanderings.

In roadways where there is no sky,
Whenever time can set him free
He leaves his subterranean world
And seeks a transient Arcady.

He weeds and waters, digs and plants,
He hoes and furrows patiently,
And finds in runner bean or rose
An infinite tranquillity.

With quiet pride, he leans upon
His docile spade and, God-like, sees
An Eden, full of onions,
Potatoes, peonies and peas.

A whiskered parsnip fills his heart
With humble, incoherent prayer
That he might go to Paradise
And grow celestial parsnips there.

Whenever time can set him free
His garden claims each hard-earned hour,
And fingers, rough to handle coal
Are soft as silk to touch a flower.

Caravans at Dawn

Blue and orange caravans, large and bright and lumbering,
Lurched along the lane today while yet the air was cool;
And all the little villages were mazed and warm with slumbering,
When caravans went by upon the road to Pontypool.

Autumn mists were in the air and all the grass was glistening,
Trees stretched out their slender arms and shook them free from rain,
And someone trilled a merry song when nobody was listening,
While all the magic cavalcade went jolting up the lane.

Where the willows wept in sleep the brook had ceased its chattering,
Every tiny wind and leaf was very, very still,
When suddenly the air was filled with clashing and clattering,
And blue and orange caravans came trundling down the hill.

Creaking wheels and cracking whips, pots and pans and crockery,
Rattled through the hamlet where folk still lay a-bed;
And flaunting gipsy girls leaned out, their eyes aglow with mockery
While old Twyn Barlwm wrapped the clouds more snugly round his head.

All the little villages were warm and mazed with slumbering,
Everything was silent and the morning air was cool,
When blue and orange caravans, large and bright and lumbering,
Made all things seem enchanted on the road to Pontypool.

Jenni Crane is a Pontypool-born BBC continuity announcer, broadcaster, TV and Radio Producer. With a BA Hons in Acting from The Italia Conti Academy, Jenni has worked on both sides of the camera. She authored BBC Radio 4 documentary *The Chaplain's Suitcase*. In 2023 she launched the Myfanwy Haycock Poetry Trail and presented *My Hill of Dreams* for BBC Radio Wales. Jenni has produced and introduced programmes: *Your Home Made Perfect* (BBC2), *Escape to the Chateau DIY* and *Penelope Keith's Village of the Year* (Channel 4). She lives in London with her husband and Cave the cat and hopes to make her own return home to live in Wales soon.

Artwork

The Madman (1933)
Washing Day (1939)
Goodbye Blackout (1945)
Reflections (1939)
Llangorse (1936)
Some Perfect Morning (1948)
Christmas Lullaby (1937)
The Folly (1937)

Acknowledgements

Thanks are due to Torfaen Museum, and to the editors of the *Western Mail*, the *South Wales Argus* and the *Free Press Pontypool*, for permission to reprint many of these poems.

Pontypool Community Council
Cyngor Cymuned **Pont-Y-Pŵl**

Discover the history and beautiful scenery of Torfaen through the eyes of Myfanwy Haycock.

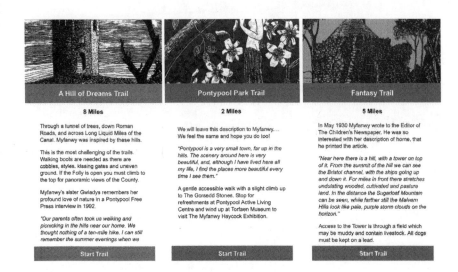

A Hill of Dreams Trail	Pontypool Park Trail	Fantasy Trail
8 Miles	**2 Miles**	**5 Miles**

A Hill of Dreams Trail — 8 Miles

Through a tunnel of trees, down Roman Roads, and across Long Liquid Miles of the Canal. Myfanwy was inspired by these hills.

This is the most challenging of the trails. Walking boots are needed as there are cobbles, styles, kissing gates and uneven ground. If the Folly is open you must climb to the top for panoramic views of the County.

Myfanwy's sister Gwladys remembers her profound love of nature in a Pontypool Free Press interview in 1992.

"Our parents often took us walking and picnicking in the hills near our home. We thought nothing of a ten-mile hike. I can still remember the summer evenings when we

Start Trail

Pontypool Park Trail — 2 Miles

We will leave this description to Myfanwy. ... We feel the same and hope you do too!

"Pontypool is a very small town, far up in the hills. The scenery around here is very beautiful, and, although I have lived here all my life, I find the places more beautiful every time I see them."

A gentle accessible walk with a slight climb up to The Gorsedd Stones. Stop for refreshments at Pontypool Active Living Centre and wind up at Torfaen Museum to visit The Myfanwy Haycock Exhibition.

Start Trail

Fantasy Trail — 5 Miles

In May 1930 Myfanwy wrote to the Editor of The Children's Newspaper. He was so interested with her description of home, that he printed the article.

"Near here there is a hill, with a tower on top of it. From the summit of the hill we can see the Bristol channel, with the ships going up and down it. For miles in front there stretches undulating wooded, cultivated and pasture land. In the distance the Sugarloaf Mountain can be seen, while farther still the Malvern Hills look like pale, purple storm clouds on the horizon."

Access to the Tower is through a field which may be muddy and contain livestock. All dogs must be kept on a lead.

Start Trail

Download the Myfanwy Trail app, choose from one of three audio trails and visit the places from which she drew poetic inspiration.

All Trails start at the Myfanwy sculpture in
The Italian Gardens, Pontypool Park.

PARTHIAN

LIBRARY OF WALES

POETRY 1900-2000: ONE HUNDRED POETS FROM WALES

Edited by Meic Stephens

The most legendary names in poetry from Wales – David Jones, Idris Davies, Vernon Watkins, R. S. Thomas, Dylan Thomas, Dannie Abse, Tony Conran, Lynette Roberts and Alun Lewis – are featured here alongside many living greats such as Gillian Clarke, Pascale Petit, Nigel Jenkins, Robert Minhinnick and Gwyneth Lewis.

Every decade of the century is featured, as is almost every part of Wales – urban, industrial and rural. Wales now has a rich, vibrant and varied literature in English and this anthology reflects it in a comprehensive, authoritative and lively way.

'This anthology is a wonderful compendium of good poems and poets worth meeting, many worth returning to again and again.'
– *New Welsh Review*

'a landmark in the English language writing of Wales.'
– *Cambria*

PB / £20.00
978-1-902638-88-1

PARTHIAN

MODERN WALES

LETTERS FROM WALES: MEMORIES AND ENCOUNTERS IN LITERATURE AND LIFE

Sam Adams

Foreword by Michael Schmidt

Edited and with an introduction by Jonathan Edwards

'Since 1996, the 'letters' have been appearing in *PN Review*, one of the most highly-regarded English literary magazines. A case can be made that they are the most significant and sustained attempt during this period to present Welsh writing to an audience throughout the UK and beyond. Their collection for the first time in this volume offers a fascinating cross-section of Welsh literary culture during this period.'
– Jonathan Edwards

'This is a huge book which serves to demonstrate the no less enormous contribution made by Sam Adams to Welsh literary life... Adams is consistently the most amiable and urbane of companions, illuminating and entertaining as he intelligently surveys the world of letters from a Welsh perspective.'
– Nation. Cymru

'In these columns, as impressive for their depth as they are for their intellectual breadth, Adams analyses the work of acclaimed Welsh writers such as Gillian Clarke, R. S. Thomas, and Rhian Edwards with scholarly panache'
– Buzz Magazine

HB / £20.00
978-1-914595-07-3

PARTHIAN *Poetry*

WILD CHERRY: SELECTED POEMS

Nigel Jenkins

Edited by Patrick McGuinness

'He became the unacknowledged national poet of his generation, an open hearted soul whose poems embodied much of what our nation is today – diverse, passionate, tender and unafraid to take a hard look at its political and cultural complexity.'
– **Menna Elfyn**

'Nigel Jenkins has a staggering presence in the literature of Wales. His poetry was both political and beautiful, deeply human, wonderfully cosmological and often scathingly humorous. Swansea's most amiable bard and, undoubtedly, its most popular poet since Dylan Thomas.'
– **Tôpher Mills**

'This selection of Nigel's work reminds us that a fine poet's voice need never be silenced.'
– **Gillian Clarke**

PB / £10.00
978-1-914595-22-6